Test Your Vocabulary – Book 1

Peter Watcyn-Jones

Illustrated by Sven Nordqvist

PENGUIN BOOKS

PENGUIN BOOKS

Published by the Penguin Group
Penguin Books Ltd, 27 Wrights Lane, London W8 5TZ, England
Penguin Books USA Inc., 375 Hudson Street, New York, New York 10014, USA
Penguin Books Australia Ltd, Ringwood, Victoria, Australia
Penguin Books Canada Ltd, 10 Alcorn Avenue, Toronto, Ontario, Canada M4V 3B2
Penguin Books (NZ) Ltd, 182–190 Wairau Road, Auckland 10, New Zealand

Penguin Books Ltd, Registered Offices: Harmondsworth, Middlesex, England

First published in Sweden by Kursverksamhetens förlag 1980
Revised edition published 1996
10 9 8 7 6 5 4 3 2

Text copyright © Peter Watcyn-Jones 1980
Illustrations copyright © Sven Nordqvist 1980
All rights reserved

Printed in England by Clays Ltd, St Ives plc
Set in Times

CONTENTS

Test√Your

Start
Testing Your
Vocabulary

PETER WATCYN-JONES

Test√Your

Vocabulary

1

PETER WATCYN-JONES

Test√Your

Vocabulary

2

PETER WATCYN-JONES

Test√Your

Vocabulary

3

PETER WATCYN-JONES

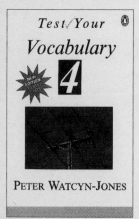

Test√Your

Vocabulary

4

PETER WATCYN-JONES

Test√Your

Vocabulary

5

PETER WATCYN-JONES

INTRODUCTION

Nowadays few people will dispute the importance of vocabulary, especially the need for active vocabulary practice. The *Test Your Vocabulary* books filled this need when they first came out, and they continue to do so. There are six books in the series, from elementary to advanced level. In this new edition of the series each book has ten new tests. To facilitate self-study there is a full Answer Key. Students using *Test Your Vocabulary* will find learning vocabulary both stimulating and enjoyable.

Test Your Vocabulary 1 is the second book in the series and is intended for elementary/lower intermediate students. There are sixty tests and approximately 900 words in the book. These are arranged into areas of vocabulary such as things in the home, clothes, jobs, holidays and festivals, shops and buildings. There are fourteen picture tests on everyday objects found in the home or at work. Finally, there are tests on synonyms, antonyms, prepositions, British and American English, rhyming words and words with more than one meaning.

TO THE STUDENT

This book will help you to learn a lot of new English words. But in order for the new words to become 'fixed' in your mind, you need to test yourself again and again. Here is one method you can use to help you learn the words.

1 Read through the instructions carefully for the test you are going to try. Then try the test, writing your answers **in pencil**.
2 When you have finished, check your answers and correct any mistakes you have made. Read through the test again, paying special attention to the words you didn't know or got wrong.
3 Try the test again five minutes later. You can do this either by covering up the words (for example, in the picture tests) or by asking a friend to test you. Repeat this until you can remember all the words.
4 **Rub out your answers.**
5 Try the test again the following day. (You should remember most of the words.)
6 Finally, plan to try the test at least twice again within the following month. After this most of the words will be 'fixed' in your mind.

1 Things in the home 1

Write the number of each drawing next to the correct word. (See example).

knife	10
vacuum cleaner	. . . . .
spoon	. . . . .
measuring jug	. . . . .
toaster	. . . . .
electric kettle	. . . . .
pair of scissors	. . . . .
fork	. . . . .
electric mixer	. . . . .
gravy jug	. . . . .

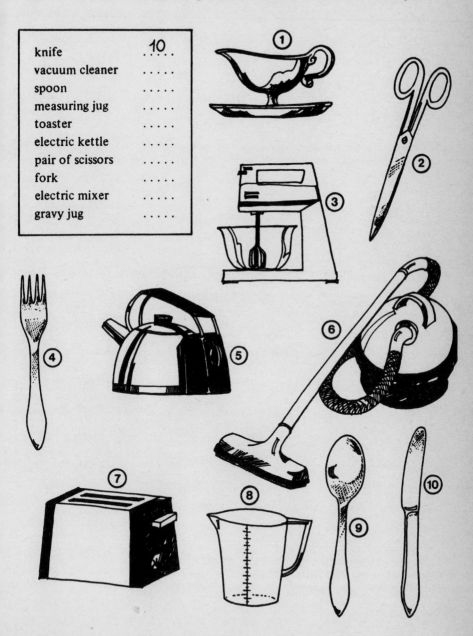

2 Synonyms – adjectives

Write down a synonym for each of the words on the left. Choose from the ones on the right. Number 1 has been done for you.

1 glad	.....happy.........	silent
2 nice	....	happy
3 wonderful	....	amusing
4 awful	....	boring
5 strange	....	rude
6 very big	....	inexpensive
7 optimistic	....	good-looking
8 funny	....	terrible
9 handsome	....	marvellous
10 dull	....	hopeful
11 impolite	....	simple
12 intelligent	....	huge
13 quiet	....	peculiar
14 easy	....	clever
15 cheap	....	pleasant

3 Countries and nationalities

Fill in the following crossword and see how many countries and nationalities you can remember.

DOWN

1 Aristotle was born in this country.
2 .... people love skiing.
3 These people make very good radios, television sets and stereos.
4 See crossword.
5 The flamenco is a typical .... dance.
6 One of the most well-known .... drinks is vodka.
7 Brigitte Bardot is ....
8 Britain was at war with this country from 1939–45.
9 A country where they eat a lot of spaghetti.
10 The .... football team lost 2–1 in the 1974 World Cup final.

ACROSS

1 This country is to the west of Spain.
2 One of the countries of Gt. Britain.
3 Hemingway's nationality.
4 This country has lots of mountains.
5 .... people drink a lot of tea.
6 The composer, Grieg, was ....
7 The capital of this country is Budapest.
8 These people eat a lot of rice.

4 Things in the home 2

Write the number of each drawing next to the correct word. (See example).

frying pan ......
grater ......
rolling pin ......
mincer ......
plate rack ......
saucepan ......
electric iron ......
casserole ......
kitchen scales ......
cruet ......
corkscrew ..8..

5 Quantities

Fill in the correct phrase under each drawing.

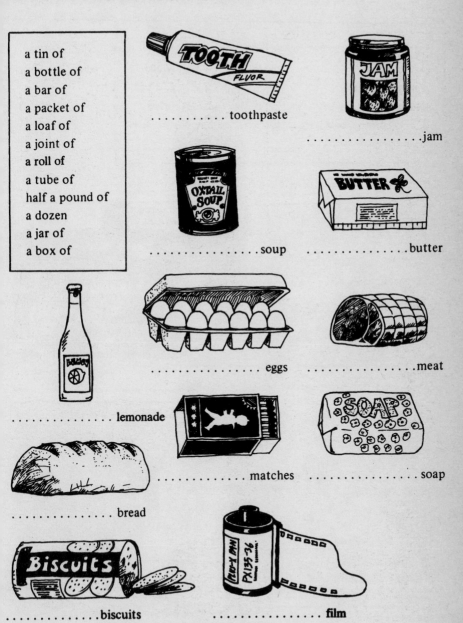

a tin of
a bottle of
a bar of
a packet of
a loaf of
a joint of
a roll of
a tube of
half a pound of
a dozen
a jar of
a box of

. . . . toothpaste

. . . . .jam

. . . . soup

. . . . .butter

. . . . eggs

. . . . .meat

. . . . lemonade

. . . . matches

. . . . soap

. . . . bread

. . . . .biscuits

. . . . film

6 Phrases 1

Fill in the missing words in the following drawings. Choose the phrases from the ones below:

a Oh, I hope not!
b It's a pleasure.
c The same to you.
d Very well, thank you.
e Congratulations!

f That's all right.
g Thank you.
h Yes, certainly.
i No, of course not.
j So do I.

7 Things in the home 3

Write the number of each drawing next to the correct word.

bathroom scales   . . . . .
radiator   . . . . .
table lamp   . . . . .
fan   . . . . .
tin opener   . . . . .
hair dryer   . . . . .
electric shaver   . . . . .
pocket calculator   . . . . .
ashtray   . . . . .
filter coffee maker   . . . . .

8 Guess their jobs

Read through the sentences and then write down which job each of the following people have.

1. MR GREEN   2. MISS EVANS   3. MR. BROWN   4. MRS WATKINS   5. MR WATSON
6. MRS SIMONS   7. MISS GEORGE   8. MR. JONES   9. MR GIBSON   10. MISS KENT

1 This person cuts men's hair. Mr Green is a b..........
2 You go to this person when you have toothache. Miss Evans is a d..........
3 You go to this person if you want a new pair of glasses. Mr Brown is an o..........
4 This person looks after you when you are flying. Mrs Watkins is an a..........
   h..........
5 This person makes sure that no one parks their car in the wrong place, or parks somewhere for too long. Not many people like this person! Mr Watson is a t.......... w..........
6 This person cuts and styles women's hair. Mrs Simons is a h..........
7 Before a house is built, this person draws the plans for it. Miss George is an a..........
8 If something goes wrong with your pipes, wash basin or bath, you usually call for this person. Mr Jones is a p..........
9 This person writes for a newspaper or magazine. Mr Gibson is a j..........
10 This person works in a library. Miss Kent is a l..........

9 Synonyms – verbs

Write down a synonym for each of the words on the left. Choose from the ones on the right. Number 1 has been done for you.

1 talk	.....speak.........	depart
2 love	....	help
3 hate	....	adore
4 fall	....	mend
5 phone	....	receive
6 swim	....	allow
7 leave	....	comprehend
8 let	....	ring
9 ask	....	loathe
10 cry	....	require
11 assist	....	weep
12 get	....	speak
13 need	....	inquire
14 understand	....	stumble
15 repair	....	bathe

10 Name the sport

Fill in the following crossword. Each answer is a different sport.

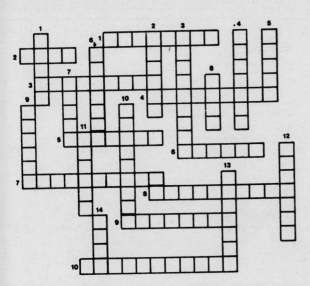

DOWN

1 Played with a ball this shape
2 Björn Borg's sport.
3 This includes things like running, jumping etc.
4 An English game foreigners find difficulty in understanding.
5 Team game — played outdoors on ice.
6 Popular winter sport.
7 English pub game.
8 Hole in one!
9 A violent sport.
10 Done in water.
11 It is dangerous to attack someone who takes part in this sport.
12 In this sport you roll something along the ice.
13 Sport on two wheels.
14 Played on horseback. Prince Charles is quite good at it!

ACROSS

1 Favourite sport in England.
2 Self-defence. A gentler form of 11 down.
3 A game similar to tennis.
4 Canada's national sport.
5 Indoor sport on ice.
6 Very fast indoor game for 2 players.
7 Both Olga Korbut and Nelly Kim won gold medals at the Olympic Games in this sport.
8 V..........
9 Could it be called football using hands instead of feet?
10 A very fast and dangerous sport.

11 Tools, etc

Write the number of each drawing next to the correct word.

screws	. . . . .
glue	. . . . .
electric drill	. . . . .
shears	. . . . .
spanner	. . . . .
saw	. . . . .
wheelbarrow	. . . . .
screwdriver	. . . . .
hammer	. . . . .
lawn mower	. . . . .
nails	. . . . .
rake	. . . . .

12 Opposites – verbs

Write down the opposite of each of the words on the left. Choose from the ones on the right. Number 1 has been done for you.

1 start	..... *finish*	arrive
2 go in	....	hate
3 find	....	come out
4 catch	....	forget
5 stop	....	fail
6 succeed	....	save
7 raise	....	demolish
8 buy	....	lose
9 depart	....	mend
10 spend	....	continue
11 love	....	drop
12 accept	....	finish
13 break	....	lower
14 construct	....	reject
15 remember	....	sell

13 Newspaper misprints

In each of the following extracts from a newspaper there is a misprint (usually a word) which completely changes the meaning of the sentence. Write down the word which is wrong and also write down which word should have been used instead.

	Misprint	Correct word
1 A thief went into the changing room at Hastings United football club. Honey was taken from the pockets of five players.	*Honey*	*Money*
2 The final practice for the children's concert will be hell on Saturday afternoon between 2.00 and 2.30.	....	....
3 Woman wanted to share fat with another.	....	....
4 The man was holding a gin as he entered the bank.	....	....
5 As well as the usual prizes, over 50 swimming certificates were presented. The school choir sank during the evening.	....	....
6 Mr Davies who was on the boat deck, ran to the rails and threw a lifeboat to the drowning man.	....	....
7 Detectives kept a witch on the house for two weeks.	....	....
8 Lady required for 12 hours per week to clean small officers at Station Road, Oxford.	....	....
9 Arsenal are hoping their new centre forward will be fat enough to play on Saturday against Manchester United.	....	....
10 All the bridesmaids wore red noses.	....	....

14 Prepositions 1

Fill in the missing prepositions in the following sentences.

1 I'm very interested .... football.
   a of   b in   c for

2 Would you like some wine .... the meal?
   a to   b for   c with

3 I'll be back .... an hour.
   a in   b for   c after

4 Is John married .... Eva?
   a by   b to   c with

5 I've been learning English .... two years.
   a for   b in   c since

6 I went to Stockholm .... air.
   a with   b on   c by

7 I bought my son a bicycle .... his birthday.
   a for   b to   c in

8 I was in the army .... the War.
   a under   b for   c during

9 He lives .... the corner of Green Street and Links Road.
   a by   b at   c with

10 Don't speak .... him now; he is not feeling very well.
   a at   b to   c with

11 Why are you .... such a bad mood today?
   a in   b on   c at

12 Where are you going .... your holidays?
   a to   b under   c for

15 Shops and buildings

On the following map are ten shops or buildings.
Read through the information below and write down the names of the different
shops or buildings.

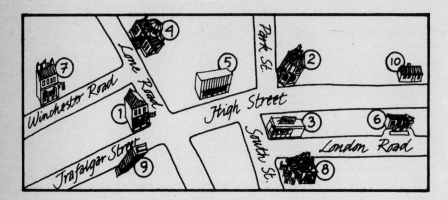

Building number 4 has lots of books in it.
The building in Trafalgar Street has 15 floors.
You can buy a bottle of wine to take home somewhere in Winchester Road.
The building at the corner of Park Street and High Street sells medicine.
Building number 9 is divided into flats.
If you are hungry, you can always go to South Street.
The Browns live in building number 10.
The building at the corner of Lone Road and Trafalgar Street is where you can
have a drink with friends.
You can buy stamps at building number 5.
Mrs Brown always shops for food in the building at the corner of South Street
and London Road. It's cheaper there!
The Browns live in a house with only one floor.
If you want petrol, go to the building in London Road.

Number 1 is a . . . .   Number 6 is a . . . .

Number 2 is a · . . . .   Number 7 is an . . . .

Number 3 is a . . . .   Number 8 is a . . . .

Number 4 is a . . . .   Number 9 is a . . . .

Number 5 is a . . . .   Number 10 is a . . . .

16 Furniture and fittings 1

Write the number of each drawing next to the correct word.

stool	. . . . .
mirror	. . . . .
Welsh dresser	. . . . .
dressing table	. . . . .
standard lamp	. . . . .
dish washer	. . . . .
roller blind	. . . . .
venetian blind	. . . . .
light switch	. . . . .
wall socket	. . . . .

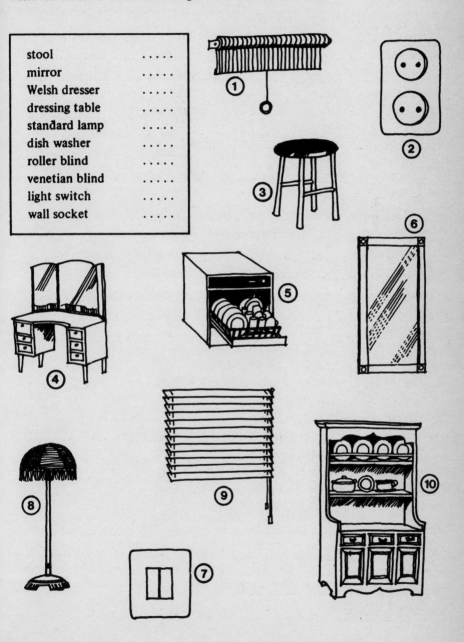

17 Choose the word 1

Write in the missing word in the following sentences.

1 When you buy something, you are usually given a ....
   a recipe   b receipt   c bill

2 You must .... for at least two hours a day if you want to play the piano well.
   a train   b practice   c practise

3 Most banks will .... people money to buy a house.
   a lend   b give   c borrow

4 I wonder if you can .... me to play the guitar?
   a assist   b teach   c learn

5 I always feel very nervous when I have to .... a speech.
   a make   b perform   c do

6 We had a very .... time in London last summer.
   a fun   b nice   c funny

7 Would you .... this letter to the Post Office, please?
   a send   b take   c bring

8 The .... in the north of Sweden is really beautiful.
   a scenery   b nature   c view

   My wife has a .... job at a chemist's.
   a half-time   b spare-time   c part-time

10 I saw a very good .... advertised in the paper this week.
   a job   b work   c occupation

11 If you put money in the bank, you get about 8% ....
   a increase   b interest   c rent

12 When I was in Denmark, I .... a boat for a few days.
   a hired   b rented   c leased

18 Food

Fill in the following crossword.

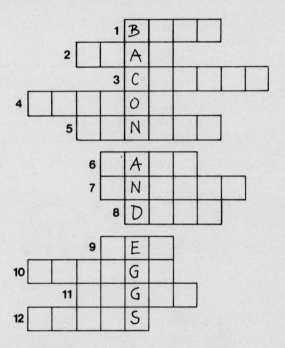

1 The meat we get from a cow.
2 The meat we get from a calf.
3 A vegetable.
4 The meat we get from a sheep.
5 A fruit.
6 Another sort of meat.
7 These vegetables make you cry!
8 A bird, often served with orange sauce.
9 The most popular drink in England.
10 Fruit. Also a colour.
11 It makes things taste sweet.
12 English people often eat fish and ....

19 Road signs

Here are 12 road signs found in England. Write the correct words under each sign.

Maximum speed limit	No entry	No overtaking
Slippery road	Keep left	No waiting
One-way traffic	Width limit	Pass either side
Two-way traffic straight ahead	Height limit	No through road

20 Parts of the body

Write the numbers 1–30 next to the correct word.

hand	. . . . .
ankle	. . . . .
navel	. . . . .
eyebrow	. . . . .
chin	. . . . .
leg	. . . . .
wrist	. . . . .
hair	. . . . .
toe	. . . . .
eye	. . . . .
finger	. . . . .
knee	. . . . .
cheek	. . . . .
forehead	. . . . .
elbow	. . . . .
ear	. . . . .
heel	. . . . .
mouth	. . . . .
nose	. . . . .
foot	. . . . .
shoulder	. . . . .
neck	. . . . .
thumb	. . . . .
palm	. . . . .
throat	. . . . .
thigh	. . . . .
arm	. . . . .
calf	. . . . .
biceps	. . . . .
Adam's apple	. . . . .

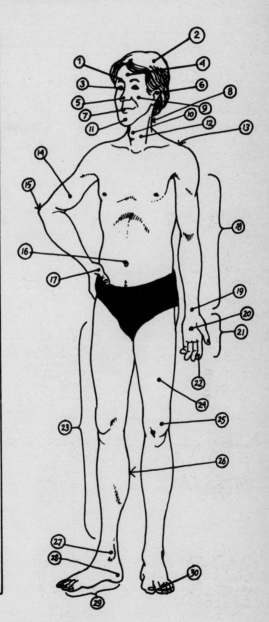

21 Furniture and fittings 2

Write the number of each drawing next to the correct word.

shelf   . . . . .
armchair   . . . . .
chair   . . . . .
footstool   . . . . .
pouffe   . . . . .
pelmet   . . . . .
chest of drawers . . . . .
wash basin   . . . . .
sink unit   . . . . .
bathroom cabinet . . . . .
cupboard   . . . . .
spotlight   . . . . .

22 Missing words – people's characteristics

Put the following words in the correct sentence.

friendly	bad-tempered	shy	patient
generous	talkative	lazy	reliable
jealous	imaginative		

1 My wife is always .... in the mornings. She gets angry at the slightest thing.

2 The thing I like about John is that he is so .... If he tells you he'll do something, then he always does it.

3 My husband is so .... He's always buying me things.

4 Paul's new girlfriend is very ...., isn't she? She hardly says a word and always looks down at the floor when she talks to you.

5 Don't ask Janina to dance – at least not if Clive, her husband, is looking. He gets so ...., you know.

6 Our new teacher is so .... If we don't understand something she goes over it again and again until we do.

7 I think English people are so .... They'll always talk to you and try to help you even if you've never met them before.

8 Pam loves to talk a lot, doesn't she? In fact, I don't think I've ever met anyone quite as .... as her.

9 Paul's wife never does any housework, even though she doesn't go out to work. I really can't understand how anyone can be so ...., can you?

10 I wish my husband were as .... as Janet's. Do you know he just makes up stories to read to the children at bedtime without the least effort. It's wonderful, isn't it?

23 Prepositions 2

Look at the plan of the boat, then fill in the missing prepositions in the sentence.

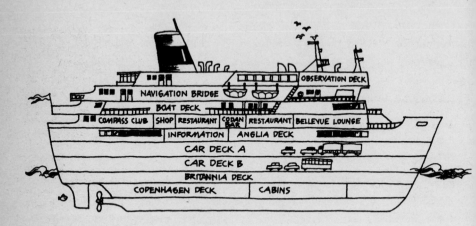

1 The Britannia Deck is .... Car Deck B.

2 The restaurant is .... the shop and the Codan Bar.

3 The Bellevue Lounge is .... the restaurant.

4 There are cabins .... the Copenhagen Deck.

5 The Observation Deck is .... the Navigation Bridge.

6 You can find your cabin number .... the Reception desk.

7 You can have a meal .... the restaurant.

8 There are steps leading .... the Observation Deck.

9 There's a rail running .... the side of the Boat Deck.

10 You have to go past the shop if you go .... the Compass Club .... the restaurant.

24 Classifications

Write one name for each of the following groups. Before starting, look at the example.

1 pig, dog, sheep, lion

2 iron, silver, copper, lead

3 shirt, tie, blouse, dress

4 wren, pigeon, thrush, eagle

5 knife, fork, soup spoon, teaspoon

6 beech, poplar, oak, willow

7 cousin, uncle, nephew, aunt

8 maize, wheat, barley, oats

9 plate, cup, saucer, bowl

10 trout, salmon, herring, cod

11 bee, ant, fly, beetle

12 motorbike, car, tram, lorry

13 crocus, daffodil, snowdrop, primrose

14 beer, milk, water, paraffin

15 saucepan, frying pan, grater, baking dish

16 violin, cello, trumpet, guitar

17 pounds, marks, yen, crowns

18 butcher, baker, salesman, tailor

19 snake, lizard, crocodile, chameleon

20 table, sofa, bookcase, chair

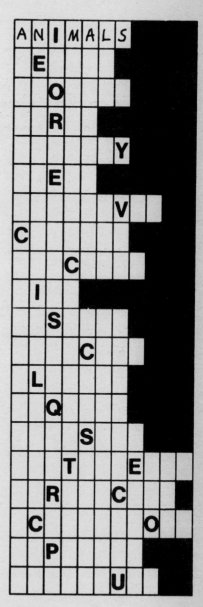

25 Complete the dialogue

In the following dialogue, the part of Jennifer has been left out. Put in the words she speaks in the right order from the phrases below.

- A bar of Lux, please.
- And a dozen eggs, please.
- Haven't you?
- A packet of crisps, please. And a bar of soap.
- Standard, please.
- Yes, please.
- Thank you. Cheerio.
- Hello, Mr Davies. I'd like half a pound of butter, please.
- And a tin of pears, please.
- No, just one more thing — a pound of cheese, please.
- All right. I'll take a tin of peaches, then.

Mr Davies: Hello, Jenny. What can I do for you?

Jennifer: ....

Mr Davies: Yes. Anything else?

Jennifer: ....

Mr Davies: Large or standard?

Jennifer: ....

Mr Davies: Here you are.

Jennifer: ....

Mr Davies: Oh, I'm afraid we haven't got any pears left.

Jennifer: ....

Mr Davies: No, but we've got lots of peaches.

Jennifer: ....

Mr Davies: Right you are. Anything else?

Jennifer: ....

Mr Davies: Yes. Now, what sort of soap do you want?

Jennifer: ....

Mr Davies: Right. Is that all?

Jennifer: ....

Mr Davies: Cheddar?

Jennifer: ....

Mr Davies: Right, then, let's see now... That's £1.51 altogether please, Jenny.

(Jennifer hands him £2)

Thank you. And 49p change.

Jennifer: ....

Mr Davies: Cheerio, love.

26 Clothes 1

Write the number of each drawing next to the correct word.

polo-neck jumper	. . . . .
jacket	. . . . .
panties	. . . . .
bra	. . . . .
suit	. . . . .
a pair of socks	. . . . .
underpants	. . . . .
shawl	. . . . .
belt	. . . . .
tie	. . . . .
skirt	. . . . .
shirt	. . . . .

27 Choose the word 2

Write in the missing word in each of the following sentences.

1 I had to keep my son home from school today because he had a ....
.... of 38.
a fever   b headache   c temperature

2 Is there anything .... you'd like me to get you?
a else   b more   c extra

3 I like going to England in the summer because it gives me a ....
.... to speak English.
a chance   b case   c possibility

4 When we were in Spain last year we .... at a marvellous hotel overlooking the beach.
a stayed   b stopped   c lived

5 My sister lives .... London.
a nearly   b near   c in the near of

6 Does your husband ever offer to do the .... ?
a washing-up   b discussing   c dishing

7 The doctor gave her a ....…..... for some medicine.
a recipe   b statement   c prescription

8 When a fire broke out in the Louvre, at least twenty ....
paintings were destroyed, including two by Picasso.
a worthless   b priceless   c valueless

9 There is a lot of talk nowadays about .... Rights.
a Humane   b Manly   c Human

10 I usually .... up at 7 o'clock in the morning.
a get   b awake   c go

11 The psychiatrist asked his patient to .... down on the couch.
a lay   b sit   c lie

12 The new musical was a great success. The .... loved it.
a audience   b spectators   c crowd

28 School report

Read through the following School report and try to write in the names of the subjects. Look at the example first.

HASTINGS COMPREHENSIVE SCHOOL		SCHOOL REPORT

Pupil's name: *Joanna Steele*   Class: **4B**

SUBJECT	GRADE	TEACHER'S REMARKS
ENGLISH	C+	Quite good, but her spelling needs to improve.
	B	Good. Her holiday in Paris has certainly helped her a lot.
	C-	Needs to work harder - especially at map reading.
	A	An excellent pupil. Very interested in the subject and her project on "Roman Britain" was the best I have ever read.
	D+	Poor. Still uses her fingers to count!
	C	Fair. A lot to learn but seems to enjoy doing experiments.
	B+	Always tries hard and is becoming an excellent tennis player.
	E	Very poor. Hates the subject - especially singing.
	C+	Quite good. Likes drawing teachers!
	B	A good pupil. Regularly does the readings at Morning Assembly.

29 Clothes 2

Write the number of each drawing next to the correct word.

pair of trousers . . . . .
scarf . . . . .
dressing gown . . . . .
duffle coat . . . . .
pair of jeans . . . . .
petticoat . . . . .
pair of "Long Johns" . . . . .
blouse . . . . .
pair of stockings . . . . .
pair of tights . . . . .
dress . . . . .
waistcoat . . . . .
raincoat . . . . .

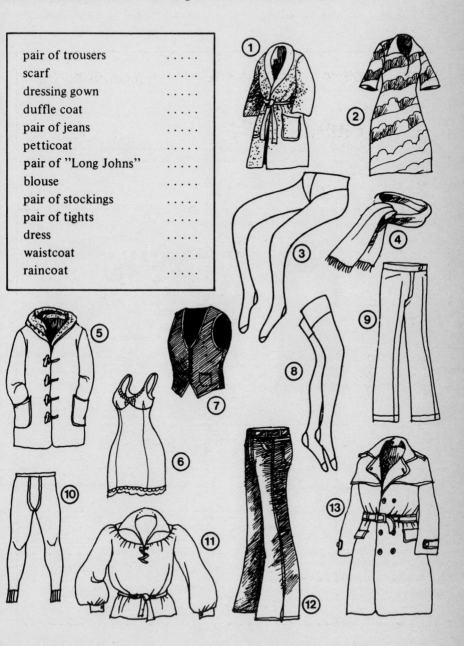

30 Phrases 2

Fill in the missing words in the following drawings. Choose the phrase from the ones below.

a Yes, please do.	f Yes, I'd be glad to.
b Oh, I hope not.	g Ah well, it can't be helped.
c Oh, what a pity!	h Yes, it is rather.
d Yes, that's right.	i Oh, how awful.
e Nice to see you, too.	j Yes, not too bad, thanks.

31 Word association

Underline two of the words on the right which are associated with or are part of the word on the left. Number 1 has been done for you.

1	TREE	brim, <u>trunk</u>, car, <u>climb</u>, cabbage
2	HOUSE	laugh, attic, forest, tongue, brick
3	BICYCLE	speak, saddle, town, pump, green
4	ORCHESTRA	go, needle, conductor, score, break
5	CHRISTMAS	pastime, decorations, lose, mistletoe, salmon
6	FOOTBALL	mole, corner, umpire, hornet, penalty
7	WEDDING	bride, storm, confetti, soap, blink
8	CAR	run, basket, clutch, boot, head
9	WAR	fight, cream, tank, apple, sincere
10	FLOWER	wren, petal, clean, buttercup, suggest
11	SCHOOL	brown, examination, dinner, offer, lesson
12	SLEEP	calm, nightmare, sheet, tongue, cushion
13	CHURCH	congregation, cough, aisle, feet, money
14	SHOE	snore, lace, heel, sit, height
15	BOOK	leaf, side, title, sheet, paperback
16	GOLF	tea, green, stick, birdie, cod
17	ENGLAND	light, Thames, garlic, pub, Edinburgh
18	FACE	heel, grin, writing, cheeks, ankle
19	TELEPHONE	switch, lure, dial, ramble, receiver
20	OFFICE	typewriter, lose, rabbit, file, perm

32 Puzzle it out

Here are five words:

CABBAGE   BANANA   CARROT   STRAWBERRY   EGG

Read through the following dialogue and try to work out which words the above are used instead of (e.g. if you think the word "egg" is used instead of "the" you write "Egg means the" etc.)

A: Excuse me, do you **cabbage** children?
B: No, I'm afraid I **banana**.
A: Oh, **carrot**'s a pity.
B: Why do you say **carrot**?
A: Because everyone should **cabbage** children.
B: Why?
A: Well, **strawberry**'s only natural.
B: I disagree. I **egg carrot** there are far too many children in the world already and I certainly **banana** want to add to the numbers.
A: **Carrot**'s a strange way to **egg**.
B: Is **strawberry**? I **egg strawberry**'s the only sensible way to look at things.
A: Well, I certainly want to **cabbage** at least four children.
B: I **egg carrot**'s a very selfish attitude to take.
A: I **banana** care! **Carrot**'s what I'm going to do.
B: Well — go ahead — **cabbage** all those children but **banana** try to tell me to **cabbage** any.
A: **Banana** worry, **carrot**'s the last thing I'd **egg** of doing.
B: I'm glad to hear **strawberry**.

CABBAGE means . . . .   BANANA means . . . .
CARROT means . . . .   STRAWBERRY means . . . .
EGG means . . . .

33 Cartoons

In the following cartoons, the captions (i.e. the words that go with a cartoon) have got mixed up so that each cartoon has been printed with the wrong caption under it. Work out the correct caption for each cartoon.

Cartoon	Correct caption	Cartoon	Correct caption
1	....	6	....
2	....	7	....
3	....	8	....
4	....	9	....
5	....	10	....

34 Fruit and vegetables

Write the number of each drawing next to the correct word.

pineapple	. . . . .
grapes	. . . . .
raspberry	. . . . .
celery	. . . . .
cucumber	. . . . .
lemon	. . . . .
corn cob	. . . . .
beetroot	. . . . .
cabbage	. . . . .
mushrooms	. . . . .
carrot	. . . . .
water melon	. . . . .
strawberry	. . . . .
cherry	. . . . .
peanuts	. . . . .
radishes	. . . . .

35 Synonyms – more adjectives

Write down a synonym for each of the words on the left. Choose from the ones on the right. Number 1 has been done for you.

1	sad	unhappy	evil
2	amusing		thrilling
3	wicked		dear
4	hard-working		unattractive
5	stubborn		witty
6	rich		furious
7	curious		wealthy
8	boring		dreadful
9	polite		industrious
10	expensive		uninteresting
11	angry		reserved
12	exciting		well-mannered
13	terrible		inquisitive
14	shy		unhappy
15	ugly		obstinate

36 Holidays and festivals

Fill in the following crossword.

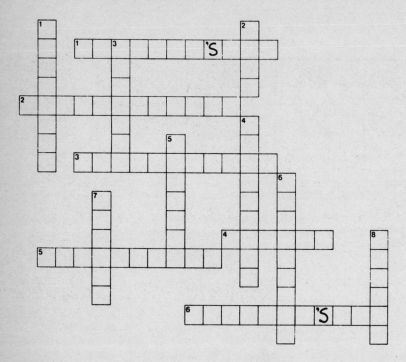

DOWN

1 Everyone has one of these days every year.
2 A .... Holiday is a special non-religious public holiday in Britain. There are usually three of these every year.
3 A religious festival in May.
4 British people call April 1st ....'s Day.
5 Most people like to relax at the ......
6 A time in Britain when people buy a lot of presents.
7 The day in the week when people go to church.
8 A religious festival in March/April.

ACROSS

1 The day when many people promise to try and better themselves by, for example, giving up smoking. (3 words)
2 The name for December 24th. (2 words)
3 I always forget our wedding ....
4 December 26th is called ...... day.
5 The day Christ was crucified. (2 words)
6 The name for December 31st. (3 words)

37 More jobs

Read through the sentences and then write down which job each of the following people have.

1. MRS SOUTH	2. MR HOPE	3. MISS BESWICK	4. MRS SHARK	5. MR GABB
6. MRS ADLER	7. MISS WOOD	8. MR GREY	9. MR SELLERS	10. MR RIGBY

1 This person is the head of a company. Mrs South is a m......... d..........
2 You meet this person when you go to church. Mr Hope is a c..........
3 You often see this person in plays on television. Miss Beswick is an a..........
4 You go to this person when you want to buy or sell a house. Mrs Shark is an
   e.......... a..........
5 This person helps run the county. Mr Gabb is a p..........
6 This person is called in to examine and report on the accounts of a company. Mrs
   Alder is an a..........
7 This person makes tables, chairs, doors, etc. Miss Wood is a c..........
8 This person makes drawings in an office – often a new design or product.
   Mr Grey is a d..........
9 He sells anything from a car to a paint brush. He usually travels a lot. Mr Sellers
   is a s.......... r..........
10 You can phone for this person if your house or flat is on fire. Mr Rigby is
   a f..........

38 Places to live

Write the number of each drawing next to the correct word.

bungalow .....
tent .....
detached house .....
caravan .....
block of flats .....
castle .....
hotel .....
semi-detached house .....
lighthouse .....
windmill .....
cottage .....
palace .....
country house/mansion .....
terraced house .....
houseboat .....

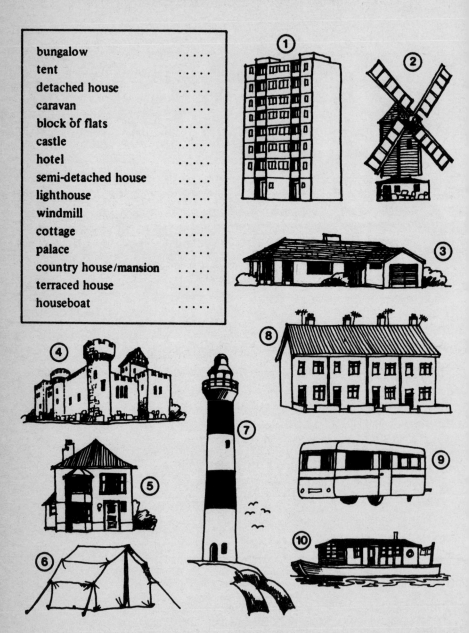

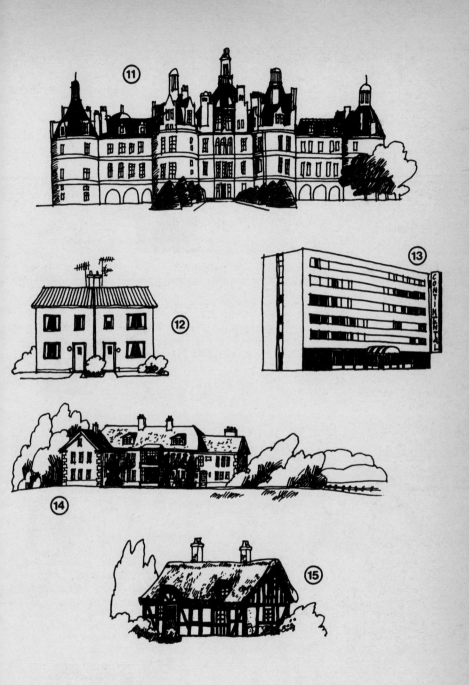

39 Match up the pairs

Fill in the missing words in the following drawings.

reader
teacher
client
policeman
bride
patient
child
employer
tennis player
dummy
guest
shopkeeper

. . . . and thief

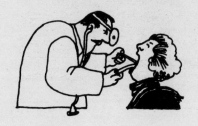

doctor and . . . .

writer and . . . .

. . . . and employee

host and . . . .

. . . . and pupil

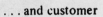
. . . . and customer   parent and . . . .

lawyer and . . . . and opponent

ventriloquist and . . . . and groom

40 Prepositions 3

Put in the missing prepositions in the following sentences.

1 My wife has just been .... Spain.
   a to   b at   c in

2 That's really typical .... John. He says he'll come but he never turns up.
   a for   b of   c to

3 I've know him .... many years now.
   a for   b since   c in

4 I must be home .... 11.30 at the latest.
   a on   b by   c at

5 My children are really looking forward .... Christmas.
   a against   b at   c to

6 Do you usually have a holiday .... Easter?
   a at   b on   c for

7 I haven't seen John .... he got married.
   a until   b since   c before

8 What time do you usually get up .... the mornings?
   a on   b at   c in

9 My son's really afraid .... dogs.
   a of   b for   c with

10 I'm afraid I'm not very good .... English.
   a in   b with   c at

11 See you .... 4 o'clock, then.
   a on   b at   c in

12 There's no point .... saving nowadays, is there?
   a to   b with   c in

41 Choose the word 3

Write in the missing word in each of the following sentences.

1 .... have you been learning English?
   a For how long time   b How long   c How long time

2 I got married .... years ago.
   a for two   b in two   c two

3 What with inflation and everything, there's just no ....
   saving nowadays.
   a idea to   b point in   c meaning to

4 You've got it all wrong, Jan. That wasn't ....
   a what I meant   b my meaning   c my purpose

5 I'm sorry but I didn't have .... to post the letters.
   a time enough   b enough with time   c enough time

6 Good morning. I .... see the manager, please.
   a will   b want to   c wish

7 Did you have .... in England last summer?
   a a nice time   b a funny time   c it very nice

8 I'm sorry, but I haven't .... today.
   a read my lesson   b done my lesson   c done my homework

9 I must remember to fill in my tax .... this week.
   a return   b declaration   c brochure

10 I thought Joanna said she .... spend the weekend with
   her parents.
   a was going to   b should   c will

11 I hate doing the .... – especially cleaning the windows.
   a homework   b housework   c jobs

12 These shoes don't .... They're much too big.
   a suit   b pass   c fit

42 Bits and pieces 1

Write the number of each drawing next to the correct word.

paintbrush	.....
safety pin	.....
ruler	.....
sewing machine	.....
pencil sharpener	.....
typewriter	.....
paper clip	.....
rubber	.....
stapler	.....
nib	.....
punch	.....
drawing pin	.....
fountain pen	.....
propelling pencil	.....
ink	......

43 Missing words – parts of a house

Put the following words into the sentences below.

upstairs	double glazing	chimney	dining room
sitting room	French windows	letter-box	hall
skylight	downstairs	cellar	gutter
landing	attic	porch	central heating

1 A house consists of two floors – .... and ....
....

2 Smoke comes out of a ....

3 The room under a house is called the ....

4 The pipe at the bottom of the roof to carry away rainwater is called the ....
....

5 You eat in the ....

6 The space under the roof, often used for storing boxes, etc. is called the ....
....

7 Most families relax and watch television in the ....

8 A window which opens out onto the roof is called a ....

9 The postman delivers letters through the ....

10 Most modern houses have .... instead of
open fires.

11 The space inside the front door (usually near the stairs) is called the ....

12 In modern houses, the windows are made up of two panes of glass instead
of just one. This is called ....

13 The space at the top of the stairs is called the ....

14 Doors made of glass which usually open out onto the garden are called ......
....

15 In some houses, there is a covered space before you go through the front
door. This is called the ....

44 Out of doors

Rearrange the letters to find out the names of the things in the following drawing.

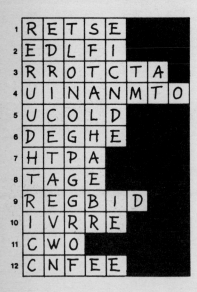
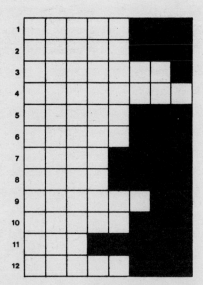

1	R	E	T	S	E	
2	E	D	L	F	I	
3	R	R	O	T	C	T	A
4	U	I	N	A	N	M	T	O
5	U	C	O	L	D	
6	D	E	G	H	E	
7	H	T	P	A		
8	T	A	G	E		
9	R	E	G	B	I	D
10	I	V	R	R	E	
11	C	W	O			
12	C	N	F	E	E	

45 Bits and pieces 2

Write the number of each drawing next to the correct word.

rubber band	. . . . .
biro/ballpoint pen	. . . . .
lighter	. . . . .
hook	. . . . .
plug	. . . . .
tap	. . . . .
penknife	. . . . .
torch	. . . . .
date stamp	. . . . .
paper-fastener	. . . . .
envelope	. . . . .
toothbrush	. . . . .
dice	. . . . .
button	. . . . .
funnel	. . . . .

46 Opposites – more adjectives

Write down the opposite of each of the words on the left. Choose from the ones on the right. Number 1 has been done for you.

1	strong	*weak*	depressed
2	generous		noisy
3	exciting		lazy
4	innocent		mean
5	quiet		poor
6	simple		smooth
7	hard-working		sober
8	careful		boring
9	deep		attractive
10	rough		complicated
11	sharp		weak
12	wealthy		careless
13	ugly		shallow
14	happy		guilty
15	drunk		blunt

47 British and American English

Write down the missing British or American words. Look at the example first.

AMERICAN ENGLISH   BRITISH ENGLISH

1 sidewalk   ..... *pavement* ....

2 ....   taxi

3 apartment   ....

4 ....   underground

5 apartment building   ....

6 ....   petrol

7 candy   ....

8 . . . . shop

9 drugstore . . . .

10 . . . . autumn

11 movie . . . .

12 . . . . lift

13 railroad . . . .

14 . . . . tram

15 parking lot . . . .

48 A family tree

Look at the following family tree and then fill in the missing words in the sentences below. Look at the example first.

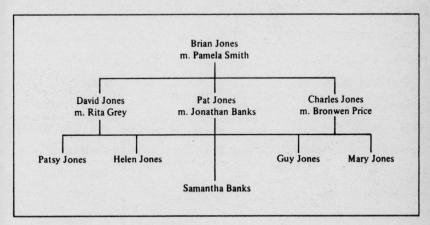

1 Brian is David's ... *father* ....
2 Patsy and Samantha are ....
3 Charles is Pat's ....
4 Bronwen is Guy's ....
5 Pamela is Helen's ....
6 Rita is David's ....
7 Jonathan is Patsy's ....
8 Charles is Jonathan's ....
9 Pamela is Bronwen's ....
10 Rita is Mary's ....
11 Jonathan is Pat's ....
12 Guy and Mary are Brian's ....
13 Brian is Bronwen's ....
14 Patsy is Helen's ....
15 Jonathan is Brian's ....
16 Guy is David's ....
17 Guy is Bronwen's ....
18 Pat and Jonathan are Samantha's ....
19 Mary is Rita's ....
20 Rita is Brian's ....

55

49 Who uses what

Complete the sentences below by choosing a suitable word from the ones on the right. (Use each word once only).

1 A crash helmet is used by	a shop assistant
2 A whistle is used by.	a teacher
3 A typewriter is used by.	a golfer
4 A palette is used by.	a businessman
5 Pins are used by.	a motorcyclist
6 A blackboard is used by	a referee
7 A chisel is used by.	a policeman
8 A tripod is used by	a doctor
9 A microscope is used by	a conductor
10 A stethoscope is used by	an artist
11 A rifle is used by.	a camper
12 A till is used by.	a dressmaker
13 An anvil is used by	a scientist
14 Handcuffs are used by.	a soldier
15 A sleeping bag is used by	a secretary
16 A tee is used by.	a fireman
17 A wheelbarrow is used by	a blacksmith
18 A music stand is used by	a photographer
19 A ladder is used by	a gardener
20 A briefcase is used by	a carpenter

50 Bits and pieces 3

Write the number of each drawing next to the correct word.

protractor	. . . . .
bracelet	. . . . .
plant	. . . . .
needle	. . . . .
hook and eye	. . . . .
candlestick	. . . . .
compass	. . . . .
set-square	. . . . .
stepladder	. . . . .
bucket	. . . . .
padlock	. . . . .
zip	. . . . .
press stud	. . . . .
pins	. . . . .
cufflinks	. . . . .

51 Choose the word 4

Underline the word which best completes the following sentences. Number 1 has been done for you.

1 His parents wouldn't (a allow b <u>let</u> c permit) him stay out later than 10.30 at night.

2 'Do you have anything to (a show up b offer c declare)?' the customs officer asked the passenger.

3 It was very difficult to see the road through the (a thick b strong c deep) fog.

4 The wasp (a bit b stung c scratched) David on the arm.

5 The dog stood in front of the fire (a waving b nodding c wagging) its tail.

6 My sister is really (a fond b interested c keen) of children.

7 'I'm sorry I'm late.'
(a 'You're welcome.' b 'The same to you.' c 'That's all right.')

8 Some students feel (a proud b embarrassed c cautious) when they make mistakes. But they shouldn't, because everybody does when they learn a new language.

9 The (a journey b travel c voyage) from London to Cardiff took three hours on the motorway.

10 This is my brother's son, Kevin. He's my favourite (a cousin b nephew c brother-in-law).

11 Two men (a kidnapped b hitch-hiked c hijacked) a plane at Moscow airport.

12 She felt very (a disappointed b shy c unfriendly) when she didn't get the job.

13 The train now (a lying b resting c standing) at platform 11 is the 14.52 to Birmingham.

14 According to statistics, drivers over fifty have (a fewer b less c lower) accidents than drivers under twenty-five.

15 Thai cooking is usually very (a heated b spicy c chilly).

16 Choose number ten – it's my (a fortune b happy c lucky) number.

17 The shopping centre was (a crowded b full c busy) of people on the first day of the sales.

18 'What do you do for a (a work b life c living)?'

19 I won't go to the party (a unless b except c but) Robert is invited too.

20 The doctor examined the patient with a (a ruler b stethoscope c barometer).

52 Compound nouns

Take a word from the box and add it to one of the words below to form a compound noun. The clue next to each word should help you. Number 1 has been done for you.

alarm	crossing	licence	pressure
attack	fever	line	race
barrier	food	penalty	rights
card	forecast	pin	token
clock	lenses	poisoning	tongue

1 junk ......*food*...... Food that is not very healthy or good for you.
2 food .... What every restaurant fears.
3 identity .... A bit like a passport.
4 pedestrian .... The safest place to cross a busy road.
5 weather .... Useful to check before you have a picnic.
6 alarm .... Wakes you up in the morning.
7 burglar .... Might prevent people from breaking into your home.
8 heart .... A common cause of death.
9 mother .... Your main language – usually the first one you learnt as a child.
10 sound .... The Concord regularly breaks this.
11 blood .... Your doctor will check this to make sure it isn't too high or too low.
12 death .... The ultimate form of punishment.
13 contact .... Some people wear these instead of glasses.
14 arms .... Countries competing to produce more and more powerful weapons.
15 driving .... In Britain you can't get one of these until you're at least seventeen.
16 rolling .... A kitchen utensil.
17 book .... Useful to give to someone as a present – especially when you don't know their taste in reading.
18 hay .... Many people suffer from this – especially in the summer.
19 assembly .... A process of manufacturing goods in a factory.
20 human .... What Amnesty International fights for all the time.

53 Group the words

Write the following words under the correct heading (five words under each).

accordion	drill	keyboard	pink	sunshine
aunt	fog	lorry	purple	tram
cello	frost	nephew	saw	tuba
coach	hail	niece	screwdriver	turquoise
cousin	hammer	oboe	snow	van
cream	jeep	orange	spanner	wife

COLOURS	RELATIVES
MUSICAL INSTRUMENTS	VEHICLES
TOOLS	WEATHER WORDS

54 Which word rhymes?

Underline the word in each group of five words below which rhymes with the word in **bold** type.

1	**bear**	beer	hair	hear	fir	hire
2	**bone**	lone	gone	none	won	sun
3	**both**	froth	though	growth	cloth	bathe
4	**cry**	say	lay	side	grey	high
5	**deer**	bear	chair	dare	clear	wear
6	**few**	low	how	knew	bow	sew
7	**hate**	weight	cafe	height	right	might
8	**home**	lame	lone	come	comb	know
9	**hot**	gout	knot	sit	note	top
10	**lost**	post	most	toast	boss	frost
11	**love**	wave	drove	dove	shave	laugh
12	**one**	phone	gone	sum	alone	gun
13	**sale**	fall	pail	wall	dial	pile
14	**sew**	dew	grew	knew	dough	flue
15	**toes**	shoes	froze	blues	colds	choose
16	**you**	show	flew	bough	hour	though

55 Right or wrong?

Is the word in **bold** type in each of the following sentences used correctly or not? If you think it is, put a tick (✔) in the RIGHT column. If you think it isn't, put a tick in the WRONG column. Say why it is wrong and then write the correct word if there is one.

	RIGHT	WRONG
1 It's **thawing**. This means the snow is melting.	....	....
2 If someone says to you, 'Oh, sorry!' – you should reply, **'You're welcome!'**	....	....
3 The thick, main part of a tree is called the **stem**.	....	....
4 If a British person sneezes, you usually say, **'Bless you!'**	....	....
5 He had a very high **hedge** around his house.	....	....
6 A **poppy** is a small dog.	....	....
7 A **parachute** is a type of hat.	....	....
8 The **landing** is found upstairs in a house.	....	....
9 Which other vegetables have you got apart from **apricots**?	....	....
10 We can't swim here – the water's too **shallow**.	....	....
11 I work for my uncle. He is my **employee**.	....	....
12 She's only seven, but she's very **great** for her age.	....	....
13 A **spider** is a common insect in most countries.	....	....
14 To make a phone call, pick up the **receiver** and dial the number.	....	....
15 Who was the person who **discovered** the telephone?	....	....
16 An **owl** is a type of bird.	....	....
17 The **daffodil** is a common British spring flower.	....	....
18 The opposite of expensive is **dear**.	....	....
19 People who are very hungry often say 'I could **eat a horse!'**	....	....
20 He bought a new **wheelbarrow** for the garden.	....	....

56 Same word – different meaning

Some words in English can have more than one meaning. Read through the pairs of sentences below and try to work out what the missing words are. Number 1 has been done for you.

1 *wave*   As the queen got out of her car she gave the crowd a big ....
The surfer was killed when he was struck by a really big ....

2 .... There was a big .... sticking up through the mattress.
My favourite season is ....

3 .... Don't ask Sheila to join the choir. She can't read a ....
of music.
My mother left a .... saying she'd popped out to the shops and
would be back soon.

4 .... In English, a sentence should always begin with a .... letter.
Is Wellington or Auckland the .... of New Zealand?

5 .... We travelled to Amsterdam by ....
This is Mr Davies, the new athletics ....

6 .... He had blue eyes and .... hair.
As a child I used to love going to the .... I really enjoyed
going on all the rides.

7 .... Our train .... at 6.30 tomorrow morning.
The lawn was covered with .... from the two beech trees at the
bottom of the garden.

8 .... The group's first single became a big number one .... all over
the world.
If you .... your finger with a hammer, it hurts.

9 .... During January and February I usually .... for the summer.
These trousers are too ...., I'll have to shorten them.

10 .... He never buys Christmas presents for anyone. He's so ....
What does this word ....?

11 .... The dog was tied to a .... in the back yard.
Don't forget to .... this letter.

12 .... You should wear red, Julia. I'm sure it will .... you.
He wore a dark grey .... to the wedding.

57 Choose the verb

Fill in the missing verbs in the sentences below. Choose from the following and make sure you use the correct tense of the verb. Use each verb once only. Number 1 has been done for you.

agree	cut	light	ride	speak
answer	deliver	live	sell	spell
ask	fail	meet	sign	spend
close	join	paint	sing	understand
cost	knock	play	smell	wear
cross	learn	post	smoke	write

1 'Do you speak French?'
   'Not very well. But I _understand_ quite a lot.'

2 'I think there's too much violence on TV.'
   'Yes, I ....'

3 The safest place to .... a busy road is at a pedestrian crossing.

4 My wife used to .... forty cigarettes a day until she stopped two years ago.

5 'Mmm. You .... nice.'
   'Thank you. It's a new perfume from Chanel.'

6 'What colour shall we .... the bathroom walls?'
   'How about blue or dark green?'

7 Could I borrow your pen please, John? I've just got to .... this document.

8 'If I .... my car, how much do you think I'll get for it?'
   'About £3,000. Maybe £3,500.'

9 .... on the door to see if there's anybody at home.

10 You have to be over eighteen to .... this club.

11 I usually .... jeans and a t-shirt at the weekend.

12 My brother has never learnt to .... a bicycle. He tried once, fell off, and has never tried since.

13 'Did you pass your exam?'
   'No, I ....'

14 Our postman .... letters very early in the morning – usually before we get up.

15 'Try to .... all the questions,' the teacher told the students before the test started.

16 Margaret .... in London now, but she was born in Dublin.

17 My cousin can .... five languages fluently.

18 We usually .... about £100 each week on food.

19 'How do you .... your surname?'
   'J – E – N – K – I – N – S.'

20 Susan .... her finger with a knife.

64

58 Anagrams

Sort out the following anagrams. Look at the example first.

Change **toga** into an animal. .....*goat*.....

1 Change **agree** into another word for keen. ....

2 Change **asleep** into a word used by polite people. ....

3 Change **beard** into something you can eat. ....

4 Change **below** into a part of the body. ....

5 Change **bleat** into an item of furniture. ....

6 Change **carthorse** into a group of musicians. ....

7 Change **chain** into a country. ....

8 Change **cheap** into a fruit. ....

9 Change **cruelty** into a word for knives, forks, etc. ....

10 Change **disease** into a popular place to go on holiday. ....

11 Change **flog** into a popular sport. ....

12 Change **flow** into an animal. ....

13 Change **hated** into something that comes to everybody. ....

14 Change **heart** into a planet. ....

15 Change **lamp** into another part of the body. ....

16 Change **recall** into one of the rooms in a house. ....

17 Change **rose** into another word for painful. ....

18 Change **super** into something you keep money in. ....

19 Change **swap** into an insect. ....

20 Change **thing** into a time of day. ....

59 Choose the adjective

Complete the sentences below with an adjective that is similar in meaning to the word in **bold** type. Choose from the words on the right.

1 A **rude** child is ....

2 An **antique** desk is ....

3 A **plump** woman is ....

4 An **astonished** person is ....

5 A **cross** parent is ....

6 A **keen** student is ....

7 A **crazy** person is ....

8 An **unoccupied** house is ....

9 A **dull** book is ....

10 An **incorrect** answer is ....

11 An **overcast** sky is ....

12 A **slender** young girl is ....

13 A **warm** person is ....

14 A **starving** child is ....

15 A **bright** student is ....

16 A **courageous** soldier is ....

17 A **dim** light is ....

18 A **brief** message is ....

19 A **difficult** task is ....

20 A **wicked** child is ....

angry
brave
cloudy
empty
enthusiastic
faint
friendly
hard
impolite
intelligent
mad
naughty
old
quite thin
short
slightly fat
uninteresting
very hungry
very surprised
wrong

60 Too many words

Replace the words in **bold** type in the following sentences with a single word. To help you, the first and last letters of the word are given. Number 1 has been done for you.

1 The window was broken **by accident**. (a*ccidentall*y)

2 It cost £2 for children to get into the exhibition and £5 for **grown-up people**. (a....................s)

3 This knife is **of no use**. It's blunt! (u....................s)

4 James translated every word **without making a single mistake**. (c....................y)

5 My **father's brother** is called Andrew. (u....................e)

6 Colin asked the pop singer for her **name in her own handwriting**. (a....................h)

7 I received a signed copy of the book from the **person who wrote it**. (a....................r)

8 Three prisoners tried to **get free** at the weekend. (e....................e)

9 Driving a car without a driving licence is **against the law** in this country. (i....................l)

10 The sun came out and soon most of the snow had **turned into water**. (m....................d)

11 Mexico City has a very high **number of people living in it**. (p....................n)

12 I **hardly ever** have a cooked breakfast. (s....................m)

13 David's parents live in a **one-storey house** near Brighton. (b....................w)

14 There are many **moving staircases** on the London Underground. (e....................s)

15 If you heat a piece of metal it will **get bigger**. (e....................d)

16 We stood in a long **line of people waiting** outside the cinema. (q....................e)

17 They set out at 8.30 in the morning and didn't **get back again** until 11.30 at night. (r....................n)

18 The population of the world has increased a lot during the past **hundred years**. (c....................y)

Answers

TEST 1

knife	10
vacuum cleaner	6
spoon	9
measuring jug	8
toaster	7
electric kettle	5
pair of scissors	2
fork	4
electric mixer	3
gravy jug	1

TEST 2

1 happy
2 pleasant
3 marvellous
4 terrible
5 peculiar
6 huge
7 hopeful
8 amusing
9 good-looking
10 boring
11 rude
12 clever
13 silent
14 simple
15 inexpensive

TEST 3

Down
1 Greece
2 Austrian
3 Japanese
4 Swedish
5 Spanish
6 Russian
7 French
8 Germany
9 Italy
10 Dutch

Across
1 Portugal
2 Wales

3 American
4 Switzerland
5 English
6 Norwegian
7 Hungary
8 Chinese

TEST 4

frying pan	10
grater	2
rolling pin	5
mincer	1
plate rack	6
saucepan	3
electric iron	4
casserole	11
kitchen scales	7
cruet	9
corkscrew	8

TEST 5

a tube of toothpaste
a jar of jam
a tin of soup
half a pound of butter
a bottle of lemonade
a dozen eggs
a joint of meat
a loaf of bread
a box of matches
a bar of soap
a packet of biscuits
a roll of film

TEST 6

1 d
2 b
3 i
4 f
5 j
6 a
7 e
8 g
9 c
10 h

TEST 7

bathroom scales	7
radiator	4
table lamp	9
fan	6
tin opener	10
hair dryer	1
electric shaver	5
pocket calculator	3
ashtray	8
filter coffee maker	2

TEST 8

Mr Green is a barber.
Miss Evans is a dentist.
Mr Brown is an optician.
Mrs Watkins is an air hostess.
Mr Watson is a traffic warden.
Mrs Simons is a hairdresser.
Miss George is an architect.
Mr Jones is a plumber.
Mr Gibson is a journalist.
Miss Kent is a librarian.

TEST 9

1 speak
2 adore
3 loathe
4 stumble
5 ring
6 bathe
7 depart
8 allow
9 inquire
10 weep
11 help
12 receive
13 require
14 comprehend
15 mend

TEST 10

Down
1. rugby
2. tennis
3. athletics
4. cricket
5. bandy
6. skiing
7. darts
8. golf
9. boxing
10. swimming
11. karate
12. curling
13. cycling
14. polo

Across
1. football
2. judo
3. badminton
4. ice hockey
5. skating
6. squash
7. gymnastics
8. volley ball
9. handball
10. motor racing

TEST 11

screws	7
glue	5
electric drill	10
shears	12
spanner	1
saw	4
wheelbarrow	8
screwdriver	2
hammer	11
lawn mower	6
nails	3
rake	9

TEST 12

1. finish
2. come out
3. lose
4. drop
5. continue
6. fail
7. lower
8. sell
9. arrive
10. save
11. hate
12. reject
13. mend
14. demolish
15. forget

TEST 13

1	Honey	Money
2	hell	held
3	fat	flat
4	gin	gun
5	sank	sang
6	lifeboat	lifebelt
7	witch	watch
8	officers	offices
9	fat	fit
10	noses	roses

TEST 14

1. b
2. c
3. a
4. b
5. a
6. c
7. a
8. c
9. b
10. b
11. a
12. c

TEST 15

1. pub
2. chemist's
3. supermarket
4. library
5. post office
6. filling-station (garage)
7. off-licence
8. restaurant
9. block of flats
10. bungalow

TEST 16

stool	3
mirror	6
Welsh dresser	10
dressing table	4
standard lamp	8
dish washer	5
roller blind	1
venetian blind	9
light switch	7
wall socket	2

TEST 17

1. b
2. c
3. a
4. b
5. a
6. b
7. b
8. a
9. c
10. a
11. b
12. a

TEST 18

1. beef
2. veal
3. carrot
4. mutton
5. banana
6. lamb
7. onions
8. duck
9. tea
10. orange
11. sugar
12. chips

TEST 19

1. One-way traffic
2. Slippery road
3. Maximum speed limit
4. Height limit
5. No through road
6. Two-way traffic straight ahead
7. No entry

8 Keep left
9 No waiting
10 Pass either side
11 No overtaking
12 Width limit

TEST 20

hand	21
ankle	27
navel	16
eyebrow	1
chin	11
leg	23
wrist	19
hair	2
toe	30
eye	3
finger	22
knee	25
cheek	9
forehead	4
elbow	15
ear	6
heel	28
mouth	7
nose	5
foot	29
shoulder	13
neck	8
thumb	17
palm	20
throat	12
thigh	24
arm	18
calf	26
biceps	14
Adam's apple	10

TEST 21

shelf	8
armchair	7
chair	12
footstool	6
pouffe	2
pelmet	5
chest of drawers	3
wash basin	9
sink unit	11
bathroom cabinet	1
cupboard	10
spotlight	4

TEST 22

1 bad-tempered
2 reliable
3 generous
4 shy
5 jealous
6 patient
7 friendly
8 talkative
9 lazy
10 imaginative

TEST 23

1 below
2 between
3 next to
4 on
5 above
6 at
7 in/at
8 up to
9 along
10 from ... to

TEST 24

1 animals
2 metals
3 clothes
4 birds
5 cutlery
6 trees
7 relatives
8 cereals
9 crockery
10 fish
11 insects
12 vehicles
13 flowers
14 liquids
15 utensils
16 instruments
17 currencies
18 occupations
19 reptiles
20 furniture

TEST 25

Jennifer's part:
– Hello, Mr Davies. I'd like
half a pound of butter, please.

– And a dozen eggs, please.
– Standard, please.
– And a tin of pears, please.
– Haven't you?
– All right. I'll take a tin of
peaches, then.
– A packet of crisps, please.
And a bar of soap.
– A bar of Lux, please.
– No, just one more thing –
a pound of cheese, please.
– Yes, please.
– Thank you. Cheerio.

TEST 26

polo-neck jumper	8
jacket	5
panties	12
bra	1
suit	7
a pair of socks	3
underpants	11
shawl	6
belt	2
tie	9
skirt	4
shirt	10

TEST 27

1	c
2	a
3	a
4	a
5	b
6	a
7	c
8	b
9	c
10	a
11	c
12	a

TEST 28

English
French
Geography
History
Maths/Mathematics
Science
(Physics/Chemistry/Biology)
Games

Music
Art
Religion

TEST 29

pair of trousers	9
scarf	4
dressing gown	1
duffle coat	5
pair of jeans	12
petticoat	6
pair of 'Long Johns'	10
blouse	11
pair of stockings	8
pair of tights	3
dress	2
waistcoat	7
raincoat	13

TEST 30

1 g
2 e
3 j
4 a
5 h
6 c
7 f
8 b
9 d
10 i

TEST 31

1 trunk, climb
2 attic, brick
3 saddle, pump
4 conductor, score
5 decorations, mistletoe
6 corner, penalty
7 bride, confetti
8 clutch, boot
9 fight, tank
10 petal, buttercup
11 examination, lesson
12 nightmare, sheet
13 congregation, aisle
14 lace, heel
15 title, paperback
16 green, birdie
17 Thames, pub
18 grin, cheeks
19 dial, receiver
20 typewriter, file

TEST 32

Cabbage means have
Banana means don't (do not)
Carrot means that
Strawberry means it
Egg means think

TEST 33

1 7
2 6
3 9
4 8
5 10
6 3
7 2
8 4
9 1
10 5

TEST 34

pineapple	8
grapes	12
raspberry	16
celery	7
cucumber	14
lemon	1
corn cob	4
beetroot	15
cabbage	6
mushrooms	2
carrot	9
water melon	5
strawberry	10
cherry	13
peanuts	11
radishes	3

TEST 35

1 unhappy
2 witty
3 evil
4 industrious
5 obstinate
6 wealthy
7 inquisitive
8 uninteresting
9 well-mannered
10 dear
11 furious
12 thrilling
13 dreadful
14 reserved
15 unattractive

TEST 36

Down
1 Birthday
2 Bank
3 Whitsun
4 April Fool
5 Weekend
6 Christmas
7 Sunday
8 Easter

Across
1 New Year's Day
2 Christmas Eve
3 Anniversary
4 Boxing
5 Good Friday
6 New Year's Eve

TEST 37

Mrs South is a managing
  director
Mr Hope is a clergyman
Miss Beswick is an actress
Mrs Shark is an estate agent
Mr Gabb is a politician
Mrs Adler is an auditor
Miss Wood is a carpenter
Mr Grey is a draughtsman
Mr Sellars is a sales represen-
  tative
Mr Rigby is a fireman

TEST 38

bungalow	3
tent	6
detached house	5
caravan	9
block of flats	1
castle	4
hotel	13
semi-detached house	12
lighthouse	7
windmill	2
cottage	15

palace 11
country house/mansion 14
terraced house 8
houseboat 10

TEST 39

policeman and thief
doctor and patient
writer and reader
employer and employee
host and guest
teacher and pupil
shopkeeper and customer
parent and child
lawyer and client
tennis player and opponent
ventriloquist and dummy
bride and groom

TEST 40

1 a
2 b
3 a
4 b
5 c
6 a
7 b
8 c
9 a
10 c
11 b
12 c
(Note: (a) rather than (c) in
number 1 since 'been' is
understood to mean the
same as the past perfect
tense of the verb 'to go' in
the sence of to go and come
back or to visit.)

TEST 41

1 b
2 c
3 b
4 a
5 c
6 b
7 a
8 c
9 a
10 a

11 b
12 c

TEST 42

paintbrush 8
safety pin 5
ruler 12
sewing machine 10
pencil sharpener 15
typewriter 1
paper clip 4
rubber 9
stapler 13
nib 2
punch 14
drawing pin 6
fountain pen 3
propelling pencil 11
ink 7

TEST 43

1   upstairs – downstairs
2   chimney
3   cellar
4   gutter
5   dining room
6   attic
7   sitting room
8   skylight
9   letter-box
10 central heating
11 hall
12 double glazing
13 landing
14 French windows
15 porch

TEST 44

1   trees
2   field
3   tractor
4   mountain
5   cloud
6   hedge
7   path
8   gate
9   bridge
10 river
11 cow
12 fence

TEST 45

rubber band 3
biro/ballpoint pen 9
lighter 13
hook 2
plug 14
tap 10
penknife 6
torch 12
date stamp 7
paper-fastener 4
envelope 1
toothbrush 8
dice 11
button 15
funnel 5

TEST 46

1   weak
2   mean
3   boring
4   guilty
5   noisy
6   complicated
7   lazy
8   careless
9   shallow
10 smooth
11 blunt
12 poor
13 attractive
14 depressed
15 sober

TEST 47

1   pavement
2   cab
3   flat
4   subway
5   block of flats
6   gasoline
7   sweets
8   store
9   chemist's
10 Fall
11 film
12 elevator
13 railway
14 streetcar
15 car park

72

TEST 48

1 father
2 cousins
3 brother
4 mother
5 grandmother
6 wife
7 uncle
8 brother-in-law
9 mother-in-law
10 aunt
11 husband
12 grandchildren
13 father-in-law
14 sister
15 son-in-law
16 nephew
17 son
18 parents
19 niece
20 daughter-in-law

TEST 49

1 a motorcyclist
2 a referee
3 a secretary
4 an artist
5 a dressmaker
6 a teacher
7 a carpenter
8 a photographer
9 a scientist
10 a doctor
11 a soldier
12 a shop assistant
13 a blacksmith
14 a policeman
15 a camper
16 a golfer
17 a gardener
18 a conductor
19 a fireman
20 a businessman

TEST 50

protractor	5
bracelet	9
plant	11
needle	15
hook and eye	6
candlestick	13

compass	1
set square	12
stepladder	6
bucket	14
padlock	7
zip	10
press stud	4
pins	2
cufflinks	8

TEST 51

1 b let
2 c declare
3 a thick
4 b stung
5 a wagging
6 a fond
7 c 'That's all right'
8 b embarrassed
9 a journey
10 b nephew
11 c hijacked
12 a disappointed
13 c standing
14 a fewer
15 b spicy
16 c lucky
17 b full
18 c living
19 a unless
20 b stethoscope

TEST 52

1 food
2 poisoning
3 card
4 crossing
5 forecast
6 clock
7 alarm
8 attack
9 tongue
10 barrier
11 pressure
12 penalty
13 lenses
14 race
15 licence
16 pin
17 token
18 fever
19 line
20 rights

TEST 53

COLOURS
cream, orange, pink,
purple, turquoise
RELATIVES
aunt, cousin, nephew,
niece, wife
**MUSICAL
INSTRUMENTS**
accordion, cello, keyboard,
oboe, tuba
VEHICLES
coach, jeep, lorry, tram,
van,
TOOLS
drill, hammer, saw,
screwdriver, spanner
WEATHER WORDS
fog, frost, hail, snow,
sunshine

TEST 54

1 hair
2 lone
3 growth
4 high
5 clear
6 knew
7 weight
8 comb
9 knot
10 frost
11 dove
12 gun
13 pail
14 dough
15 froze
16 flew

TEST 55

1 Right
2 Wrong (you reply,
'That's all right.' You
say, 'You're welcome'
when someone thanks
you for something).
3 Wrong (it is called the
trunk; the stem is the
main part of a flower).
4 Right
5 Right (it is a type of

fence made of small
bushes).

6 Wrong (a poppy is a
bright red wild flower; a
young dog is called a
puppy).

7 Wrong (you wear it
when you jump from a
plane; it opens out and
lets you land without
killing yourself).

8 Right (it is the space at
the top of the stairs).

9 Wrong (an apricot is
not a vegetable; it is a
fruit).

10 Right (the opposite is
deep).

11 Wrong (you are the
employee; your uncle is
your employer).

12 Wrong (it should be *big*
for her age).

13 Right (it has six legs
and spins a web).

14 Right (it is the part of
the phone you hold to
your ear and speak into).

15 Wrong (it should be
invented the telephone;
you *discover* something
that is already there, e.g.
a mountain, a planet,
etc).

16 Right (it has big eyes
and usually hunts at
night for mice and other
small creatures).

17 Right (it is yellow and is
the national flower of
Wales).

18 Wrong (dear is another
word for expensive; the
opposite is cheap or
inexpensive).

19 Right

20 Right (it is a type of
cart with one wheel at
the front and two han-
dles at the back; you
push it along and use it
to carry things).

TEST 56

1 wave
2 spring
3 note
4 capital
5 coach
6 fair
7 leaves
8 hit
9 long
10 mean
11 post
12 suit

TEST 57

1 understand
2 agree
3 cross
4 smoke
5 smell
6 paint
7 sign
8 sell
9 Knock
10 join
11 wear
12 ride
13 failed
14 delivers
15 answer
16 lives
17 speak
18 spend
19 spell
20 cut

TEST 58

1 eager
2 please
3 bread
4 elbow
5 table
6 orchestra
7 China
8 peach
9 cutlery
10 seaside
11 golf
12 wolf
13 death
14 Earth
15 palm
16 cellar
17 sore
18 purse
19 wasp
20 night

TEST 59

1 impolite
2 old
3 slightly fat
4 very surprised
5 angry
6 enthusiastic
7 mad
8 empty
9 uninteresting
10 wrong
11 cloudy
12 quite thin
13 friendly
14 very hungry
15 intelligent
16 brave
17 faint
18 short
19 hard
20 naughty

TEST 60

1 accidentally
2 adults
3 useless
4 correctly
5 uncle
6 autograph
7 author
8 escape
9 illegal
10 melted
11 population
12 seldom
13 bungalow
14 escalators
15 expand
16 queue
17 return
18 century